CHI

9/06

FRIENDS
OF ACPL

ALLEN COUNTY PUBLIC LIBRARY

3 1833 05054 7170

Feeling Better

D0907636

Feeling Better

A Kid's Book About Therapy

BY *Rachel Rashkin*

ILLUSTRATED
BY *Bonnie Adamson*

MAGINATION PRESS
WASHINGTON, D.C.

For Marmy, LR, and all the children and therapists
who have the gift of journeying together.
— R.R.

To Michael, Jenny, Steffie, and Mollie.
— B.A.

Copyright © 2005 by Magination Press. All rights reserved.
Except as permitted under the United States Copyright Act of 1976, no part of this publication may be reproduced or distributed in any form or by any means, or stored in a database or retrieval system, without the prior written permission of the publisher.

Published by

MAGINATION PRESS

An Educational Publishing Foundation Book

American Psychological Association

750 First Street, NE

Washington, DC 20002

For more information about our books, including a complete catalog, please write to us, call 1-800-374-2721, or visit our website at www.maginationpress.com.

Editor: Darcie Conner Johnston

Designer: Michael Hentges

The text type is Perpetua

Printed by Worzalla, Stevens Point, Wisconsin

Library of Congress Cataloging-in-Publication Data

Rashkin, Rachel.

Feeling better : a kid's books about therapy / by Rachel Rashkin ; illustrated by Bonnie Adamson.

p. cm.

ISBN 1-59147-237-7 (hardcover : alk. paper) — ISBN 1-59147-238-5 (pbk. : alk. paper)

1. Child psychotherapy — Juvenile literature. I. Adamson, Bonnie. II. Title.

RJ504.15R37 2005

618.92'8914—dc22

2004022727

10 9 8 7 6 5 4 3 2 1

Dear Reader,

Life can be hard, especially now, when your life is changing so fast and demands from school, friends, family, and the world are getting more complicated.

It's not unusual for kids to get sad or angry, and yet not know why. It's a confusing time. Sometimes they lose interest in their friends and the activities that they used to love. They might have problems in school, or with eating, or sleeping. They might have fears that make it hard for them to do normal things. They might seem like different people to those who know and love them. They might even feel like a different person to themselves.

At such times, one tool that can help kids feel less confused and more like themselves again is psychotherapy. In therapy, kids can talk about fears, anger, loneliness, and anything else on their mind with someone who is an expert in making sense out of feelings. There is no such thing as a right or a wrong feeling; a therapist's job is to help a person understand and respect any feelings and to help him or her find the best way to express them. As people get better at knowing their feelings, they usually start to feel a lot better.

Feeling Better is a book about what happens in therapy: all the reasons why all kinds of people go to therapy, what a therapist is and what a therapist does, what kids do during a therapy session, what it feels like to be in therapy, the privacy of therapy sessions, how long it lasts, and how therapy ends. This book will help you know what to expect at every step along the way.

I hope this information helps and that you are feeling better very soon!

Rachel Rashkin

Hello, Journal. My name is Maya, and I am twelve years old. I got this journal for my birthday from my friend Darya. That's me in the picture, the one who's grinning and doing the OK signs with both of my hands. Or at least, that used to be me. Lately I haven't felt so much like that person.

I used to love hanging out with my friends— I even used to get in trouble for talking and laughing with them so much in Mr. McAllister's class. But now I don't feel so much like being with them. It's been really hard to pay attention to what my teachers say in class, ever since I started sixth grade. Most of the time I just feel like putting my head down on my desk.

I don't even care about jumping on the trampoline in PE anymore. You have to understand I LOVED the trampoline. But now I feel too tired.

Sometimes I feel okay, but mostly I feel grumpy. My stomach hurts and I get headaches, way more than I used to. And all the fun things I liked to do don't seem so fun anymore. Sometimes my friends say I seem different. Once Mr. McAllister said something too, and I was so embarrassed.

Darya and Annie are my best friends, and even they say that I act weird. They say things like, "You always look so sad. Why don't you ever want to be with us?" I try to pretend that I feel okay, but I feel like crying when they say stuff like that. It made me realize that I do feel very sad inside. But I don't understand why, and that is scary.

I feel crabby at home too. Today Mom asked if I wanted to help her bake my favorite cookies (peanut butter), but I just wanted to stay in my room. When it was time for soccer practice, I did not want to go, and I told my parents I want to quit the team. Then, when Dad told me to do my homework, I got really mad and said things I shouldn't have. And that was just today!

Yesterday was a bad day too. My little sister Leila asked me to braid her hair, and I yelled at her in a really nasty voice to go away and leave me alone. She looked at me like I was a monster or something, and

after she ran out of my room,
I felt like such a jerk. I didn't
mean what I said.

I act like I want to be alone,
and I feel like I want to be alone,
but I also feel like I really don't
want to be alone at all. I wish
someone would help me
understand what is going on
in my head. I'm scared that
I'm going to be alone for real and that nobody will
ever be able to help me.

3 1833 05054 7170

Dad came into my room last night and said, "Let's have a chat," and he brought this little wooden box with him. "What's the box for?" I wanted to know. I was kind of nervous. You always think you're in trouble when your parents say they want to talk, even if they're using a nice voice.

But Dad surprised me. I wasn't in trouble at all. Instead he started talking about feelings.

He said that sometimes, when kids are really sad or afraid or angry, and they don't know how to show those feelings or they are scared to, it's like they stuff them away in a box and try to forget the feelings are there. Even good feelings like happiness and excitement might wind up in the box, too. Dad said that when kids try so hard not to feel anything, the box gets full

and then they can get stomachaches and headaches and feel tired and grumpy.

I felt my face getting hot.

Dad also said that people need to be able to let their feelings out in the right ways, so that they can understand the feelings and then feel better. Everyone has confusing feelings now and then, but when the feelings last a long time and start to make kids act and think in different ways than usual, it might be a good idea to get help.

Then Dad told me something rather interesting. He said that when he was a boy, HE had a box that was filled with big feelings. But he never had the chance to open up his box when he was a kid, and he says he forgot all about the confusing feelings until he became an adult. His box stayed shut for such a long time that it was

very hard for him to remember why he put the feelings there in the first place!

When he was grown up, he would get angry about a lot of things, but he wasn't sure why. He said that's what can happen when feelings get buried in a box for a long time.

Dad said he needed help understanding his angry feelings and figuring out how to deal with them, so he went to a doctor called a therapist. He said he began to feel much better. Then he asked me if I wanted to go to a therapist and learn how to get my feelings out, just like he used to.

Somehow I knew that was coming.

The idea of going to a therapist makes me a little nervous. Actually, it makes me a lot nervous. I mean, who are therapists, and what do they do, and what would I have to do with one of them?

But I feel kind of relieved. I'm glad that Dad had his "chat" with me. I don't feel so alone now, and I feel like things are probably going to be okay.

Mom and Dad made me an appointment with Dr. Madison for next Wednesday after school. Before then, I'm trying to find out as much as I can about therapists. Here's what I know so far:

1. A therapist is someone who helps kids understand all the feelings going on inside of them. What you do is talk about what's going on in your life and about all your feelings when you see a therapist.

2. To be a therapist, Dr. Madison had to go to school for many years, and she has a lot of experience working with many different kinds of problems people have.

3. If you need help from a therapist, it doesn't mean you are bad or weak or dumb. It means you're smart because you want to get better.

☆4 Mom said kids see therapists for all kinds of reasons. She said in a lot of ways it's just the same as needing to see doctors and dentists for ear infections or sprained ankles or cavities. You might need a therapist if you're having trouble at school, if someone you love dies, if you see or hear something terrible happen, or if you get scared at night. Some kids might even see a therapist if they're having a hard time living in a new neighborhood, or getting used to a new brother or sister or their grandparent moving in with them.

☆5 Therapists don't help just kids. They also help moms, dads, and anyone else. There might even be times when a whole family goes to see a therapist together.

On Wednesday when I had my first appointment with Dr. Madison, I was so jumpy. What if she doesn't like me? What if she gets mad at me or tries to make me do things I don't want to do?

When Dad took me to Dr. Madison's office, he said the important thing was if I liked her, not if she liked me! He said people might try a couple of different therapists before they find one who they like, and that's okay. It's important to find just the right person who can help you feel safe and comfortable while you begin to talk about your feelings.

Dr. Madison is a woman. Dad asked me if I had any feelings about seeing a man or a woman therapist, because I had a choice. I didn't know the answer to that, because I was just nervous about the whole idea of seeing any kind of therapist, period.

I asked Dad how often I would have to see Dr. Madison, and he said Dr. Madison would decide that with me (if I like her). People might go once or twice a week, and they might need to go just a few times total, or for a few months, or for longer. Everybody's different, and the reasons people go are different. Some reasons don't need much time, and some reasons needs lots of time.

Probably the biggest thing I wanted to know, though, was if Dad would be with me when I saw the therapist. He said maybe for a few minutes today, but after that it would be just me and her, unless there was a special reason for him or Mom or anyone else to be there sometime.

Dr. Madison had a little waiting room with a pretty couch and a couple of chairs. Nobody else was there. There were some cool pictures of the ocean on the wall, and there was a little machine making sounds like wind blowing. Dad smiled. He said that when he saw his therapist, they played a radio in the waiting room. It's to make sure that when you're talking to your therapist no one in the waiting room can hear what you're saying.

Then I started feeling totally nervous. And right then is when this lady opened a door and stepped in to the room and said, "You must be Maya. I'm Dr. Madison." She looked nice, and kind of reminded me of my Aunt Beth, who is my mom's sister and my most favorite relative. I wasn't so scared all of a sudden.

She said hello to my dad and asked if he would like to wait while she talked to me and that she would like to ask him in at the end of our session. So that answered that.

Before I had a chance to get really nervous again, Dr. Madison asked me to come in and sit down. She said to make myself comfortable. There were a couple of places to choose from. I picked a cozy looking couch that had puffy yellow and blue pillows.

The first thing she said was that what we talk about in this room is private, just between her and me. It's called confidentiality, and it means I can feel safe telling her anything, like what I dream about at night, what I love and what I hate, or what I wish for, and she won't tell anybody.

She did say there might be

times, though, when I would want help sharing something important with another adult or kid, and that she could help me find a way to do that. For instance, she said that sometimes if a kid's behavior in school has been different than it usually is, the teacher might need to know that the kid is in therapy so the teacher can understand how to help.

She also said that even though just about everything you talk about is between you and your therapist, there might be things you talk about that will be too big for both of you to keep private. If other people are hurting you, or if you feel like hurting yourself, part of a therapist's job is to protect you by letting someone else know what is going on so that you stay safe. That doesn't mean she is being a tattletale or breaking the rule of confidentiality. In fact, if you

 tell your therapist something that another adult needs to know about, the two of you can talk ahead of time about what it might feel like to have someone else know the information.

After all that, Dr. Madison asked me a few questions about school and if I like it, and how old I am, and who is in my family, stuff like that. She seemed really interested, but not in a pushy way—like she just cared. Then she said it was time to ask my dad in. When he sat down, she told us both that she thought she could help. That seemed fine to me.

 So we agreed that I would come back next Monday at 4:00.

Every Monday, Mom or Dad picks me up from
school and takes me to my session with Dr.
Madison. They stay in the waiting room with the
wind machine going, reading a book or something.
Dr. Madison always comes in to the waiting
room and smiles and says, "Hello, Maya.
C'mon in!"

   Her office is full of cool stuff.
She has fun games and art
supplies to make things with.
There's also a big sand tray in the middle of
the room, and she has all kinds of puppets and little
people and animal dolls that I can use to make up
plays with. On the walls there are more
paintings like the ones in the waiting
room—nature pictures like the ocean
and a forest and a sunset, which I

like to look at when I am thinking. There is even a waterfall statue on her desk that helps me feel relaxed. I usually sit on the same couch, because I like to hold the pillows while we're talking.

Dr. Madison is nice, and she's also funny. Most of the time I think she's really cool and I like seeing her. We talk about things that are happening in school, or what kinds of things I like to do with my friends or by myself. Sometimes if I feel stuck about what to talk about, she asks me if I want to play a board game together or use water- colors and paint pictures.

Yesterday I was feeling kind of sad, and Dr. Madison asked me if I wanted to try to paint a picture of the sadness. I was surprised! It was kind of cool having to imagine what sad feelings look like and then getting to paint them. It ended up looking like a drawing of a thunderstorm. Dr. Madison and I spent the rest of the session talking about my picture and what it was like to begin understanding some of my sad feelings. I felt a lot better after that.

Therapy is going okay. But there are some Mondays when I feel crabby or had a bad day at school, and I would rather come home and do other things, like play on the computer or practice rollerblading. I don't always feel like smiling or going inside the room with Dr. Madison. Mom says it's okay to feel anxious or grumpy before your session. Dad says that it takes a lot of work to keep your box of feelings shut, and knowing that your therapist will help you open it up can sometimes make you feel nervous or even mad.

On those days, my mom or dad usually

reminds me how important therapy is and that each time I go, I am getting better. Sometimes I get annoyed when they say that again and again, but I know they are right and that I am getting better. Even when it feels like I'm not.

That's the funny thing about being in therapy. You go to help solve your problems and feel better, but sometimes you actually start to feel worse! Mom says that it's totally normal to feel really overwhelmed, especially in the beginning, and that learning about your feelings can be kind of like learning to speak a whole new language.

That reminded me of when we went to Spain last summer. There were all these new sounds and words around me, and it was really hard to understand what it all meant. But after a while, I could recognize different words, and then I wasn't so afraid to try to speak Spanish myself.

I guess that's how therapy is. It seems like everything you're feeling is so hard to understand at first, and it's frustrating when you aren't really sure what the things you're thinking and feeling and sometimes even saying mean! But the more you keep going and talking about your problems, the more you understand them and feel better.

I've been thinking about telling one of my friends that I'm in therapy, but I'm kind of nervous about it. Dr. Madison said it's my decision whether or not to tell any of my friends. When kids don't really understand something, they might say mean things, and some kids might have some wrong ideas about what therapy is.

I did it! I was a little scared to tell anyone at first, but after a while I decided to tell Annie and Darya so they would understand a little better why I didn't always feel like playing.

At first Annie made a joke about me being crazy. I was kind of hurt and it made me mad, but I remembered that Dr. Madison said that kids might not have any idea what therapy was like. So I just said it's not like that, and told her what I do with Dr. Madison and how I'm feeling so much better. She was really interested, in a good way. She even said that she wished she

could talk to Dr. Madison about a couple of her own problems.

I got a big surprise when I told Darya. Her parents were divorced last year, and her dad and brother moved away so she doesn't see them much at all. Of course, I already knew that. What I didn't know was that she has been seeing a therapist to help her deal with missing them and with being sad and angry about what happened to her family!

Also, she said she has a cousin who would get so creeped out by insects that he had a hard time going outside or anything. So his parents took him to see a therapist who taught him all about bugs and even helped him learn to hold one. (Yuck!)

It felt so good to know that I wasn't the only one. And it feels totally great to be able to talk to my friends about therapy, especially one who knows exactly what it's like.

When I tell Dr. Madison about what's going on, she usually asks me questions about how I feel about this or that. She says she wants us to be able to figure out why I feel so alone sometimes, or tired, or angry. Lots of times I can't think of anything to say, and nothing at all comes out of my mouth.

Once I told Dr. Madison I thought this was really boring, and she said if you feel bored during your session, it could mean that you're working especially hard to ignore your feelings. Dad would say you're trying to keep your box of feelings shut tight. She said she can help me understand why I would rather not talk about them. When I don't feel like talking, doing artwork is one good way to help us figure out what's going on inside my head. I use my imagination and think about what it is I'm feeling and then I draw it. It's kind of like taking all the words that are jumbled up in my head and turning them into a picture. Then Dr. Madison and I look at my picture, and we talk about how it might be connected to what I'm feeling inside.

It also helps to play with the sand or with clay. A few sessions ago when I didn't feel like talking, I made an airplane out of blue and yellow clay. Afterward, Dr. Madison and I talked about why I chose to make an airplane instead of something else. I wasn't sure at first, but then we talked about how some people fly on airplanes when they travel to places. I started to learn that part of why I was having problems was because my mom has a new job and she has to travel a lot.

 When my therapist and I began to talk about what it felt like when my mom goes away on trips, I started to cry. I was embarrassed to cry in front of her, and I tried hard not to. But she said it's totally okay to cry and gave me a box of tissues. And I felt so much better after I did!

It was so cool when I started to realize that how I was feeling at home and at school had a lot to do with Mom going away so much. It's amazing that when you start to understand your big feelings, things start to make more sense.

So in the car, I told Mom that I miss her when she goes away. We had a great talk about how we can talk more on the phone or email each other when she is gone. We also decided that the day before she has to go, we'll spend some extra time

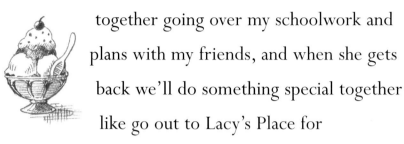

together going over my schoolwork and plans with my friends, and when she gets back we'll do something special together like go out to Lacy's Place for an ice cream and catch up on what happened while she was away.

Therapy really is helping! I feel so much better, like it's spring or something! When you know what's going on in your head, you can do something about it, and it feels awesome!! It really feels like my problems are getting smaller and smaller.

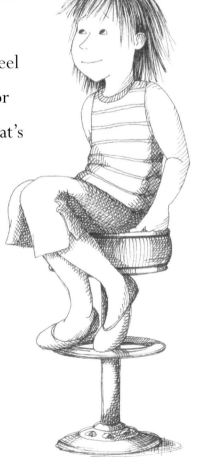

Boy, I thought math homework was difficult, but sometimes Dr. Madison asks me questions or says things that make me have to think so hard it almost hurts! Her questions can even make me feel really mad! When that happens, I don't want to do anything. I don't want to answer her or make anything with the art supplies. I don't even want to look at her. Sometimes I actually want to yell at her to just go away and leave me alone.

When that happens, Dr. Madison says feeling angry is normal and that even though

 it might feel embarrassing or scary, we can find safe ways to understand my angry feelings.

It can be pretty hard to find the right words when you have strong feelings, but Dr. Madison helps. Once when I was angry, I hit a pillow hard and shouted, "I'm so mad that my mom is gone again!" That surprised me—finding out that it wasn't really Dr. Madison that I was mad at. I felt better when I figured out what was bothering me.

At the end of my sessions, Dr. Madison smiles at me and says, "Bye, Maya, see you next week."

Just like you can have lots of different feelings at the beginning of your session, I've found out all sorts of feelings can happen at the end too. If you're having a lot of fun and feeling comfortable talking, it's disappointing to have to leave.

One thing that helps is I can take home anything I've created during the session. Bringing something home from Dr. Madison's office is a great way to remind myself that I'll be seeing her again soon.

On the other hand, sometimes I really want to get out of there because I wasn't in the mood to talk about my feelings that day. There are times when I feel so mad at the end that I practically stomp out of the room and don't ever want to come back. Those are the times when I really have to think after I get home, to try to figure out why I feel so mad.

There are lots of things I do to help myself feel better and make sense of things. I paint or draw pictures, go rollerblading, call Darya or Annie, or write in this journal. Sometimes I feel like talking to Mom or Dad about it, and they mostly just listen, which is great. They don't try to tell me not to be upset.

I know the upset feelings won't last forever, and that it's part of getting to know myself better. And that I'll be ready to see Dr. Madison again the next week.

May 27

Dr. Madison is on vacation
so I don't have therapy
for two weeks. I'm so
glad that I have a ther-
apist like her. Some-
times it almost feels
like she's a good friend or my aunt or something. I
kind of wish sometimes that she was my mom. Of
course, I don't really want her to be my mom, but
sometimes I wish she could do mom-like things,
like come to one of my soccer matches, or go out

for ice cream with me. Especially when Mom is away.

I never thought that my therapist would be someone I would miss a lot, or someone I would think about, or someone I'd get mad at and yell at! I remember in the beginning when Dad first came into my room with that box and we had our chat about big feelings. When he mentioned the idea of me seeing a therapist, it was so hard to imagine what it would be like. But now, I wouldn't trade it for anything.

Seeing Dr. Madison each week has helped me so much. She doesn't ever yell at me or get mad about stuff, and she doesn't judge me, either. I can tell her that I didn't do any of my homework or that I moped around in my room instead of going with Annie and Darya to see a movie, and she doesn't ever criticize me or tell me what she thinks I should have done. Instead, she just talks to me, and she always acts like she really cares about me.

It's weird, but with Dr. Madison on vacation now, it kind of makes me miss her in the same ways I miss Mom when she goes away on business trips. At first when Dr. Madison said she was going to be gone, I felt funny about it. I didn't say anything then, but the next time I saw her I told her that this reminded me of Mom going away. She said she was really glad that I told her, and she was impressed that I noticed that it reminded me of Mom. That made me think about the talks Mom and I have had, and how things have gotten so much better when she has to take a trip. And that made me feel better about Dr. Madison being gone.

I can't wait for her to come back!

I can't believe I'm in seventh grade and that I've been seeing Dr. Madison for almost a year! I asked her when I would stop coming for my sessions, and she said we would decide together when it's time.

I've noticed that I haven't been so grumpy for a long time, although I still have some crabby days, but Mom and Dad say that's just normal for everyone. I definitely don't feel so sad or overwhelmed the way I used to. I've found lots of ways to help myself when I'm feeling anxious, or afraid, or mad. And the things that used to bother me a lot don't bother me so much, now that I have figured out why I feel the way I do and how to handle my feelings better. Darya and Annie said it's like the old me is back! That felt GREAT to hear! Too bad Mr. McAllister can't see me now!!

But I'm still not so sure I'm ready for my therapy to end. Dr. Madison says it's okay to feel that way, and that lots of times people

don't feel 100 percent ready. Sometimes you know you're ready, but you just like coming and talking, so you don't want to say goodbye.

Lately we've spent most of our time talking about how much I've learned about myself and the new skills I have for handling big feelings that might come up. It feels terrific, knowing that I can handle things so much better on my own now. But it still feels sad that I'll have to say good-bye to Dr. Madison.

Dr. Madison says that all kids need help from their parents and other adults sometimes, and that's fine. She said I may have noticed that adults need help from each other sometimes too. It's all part of being human—it connects us together and makes us healthy and strong, and it's something to celebrate. I never thought of it that way! She says that I always have someone to turn to when I need help. Also, if

I ever need to, I can always come back to therapy.

Being in therapy can be fun and exciting, and it can also be hard work and feel a little scary or make you mad. But you end up feeling really proud of yourself for working through your big feelings. I learned to like school again, and I want to be with my friends, and do all the things I used to enjoy. Most of all, though, I learned that it's okay to need help, and that even though in the beginning I was embarrassed and scared about seeing a therapist, now I realize that it was a very smart decision and I'm glad I stuck with it.

I think I'll be ready to stop going to therapy very soon.

About the Author

Rachel Rashkin has an M.S. in child development from the Erikson Institute for Child Development. She writes parenting articles and self-help stories for children and is creating a website for kids about psychotherapy (www.helpingkidsheal.com). In her spare time, she performs in musical theater and has taught music and movement for young children, and she bakes bread. Rachel lives in Chicago.

About the Illustrator

Bonnie Adamson finds illustration a welcome change of pace from an increasingly computer-driven career in graphic design. She lives in Greenville, South Carolina, with her husband and faithful assistant, Mollie-the-Dog. Two grown daughters who provided years of invaluable insight into the mysteries of childhood continue to offer encouragement and inspiration, and occasionally recognize them-selves in their mother's drawings.